SUPERMAN

AND THE SHOWDOWN AT SATURN

A SOLAR SYSTEM ADVENTURE

by Steve Korté
illustrated by Gregg Schigiel

Superman created by Jerry Siegel and Joe Shuster
by special arrangement with the Jerry Siegel family

Consultant:
Steve Kortenkamp, PhD
Associate Professor of Practice
Lunar and Planetary Lab
University of Arizona
Tucson, Arizona

CAPSTONE PRESS
a capstone imprint

The mighty hero Superman has just arrived at the world-famous scientific laboratory known as S.T.A.R. Labs. Professor Emil Hamilton asked the Man of Steel to come right away.

"Something unusual has happened," says Hamilton. He brings up an image on a large video screen. "Years ago, we launched this spacecraft to orbit Saturn and take photographs. But today it stopped sending images."

"Perhaps it was hit by an asteroid?" suggests Superman.

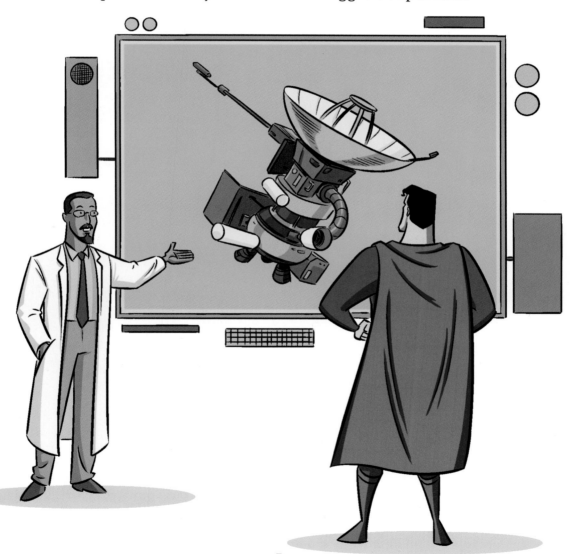

"I'm afraid it was no asteroid," says Hamilton. He punches a button on a keyboard. "This was the final image from the spacecraft."

Superman gasps as he looks at the screen. It shows a large hand grabbing the spacecraft's camera lens.

"Something—or someone—has damaged our spacecraft," says Hamilton.

"Professor, I need to find out what happened," says Superman. "I'm going to Saturn."

Minutes later, Superman soars into space. He has a very long journey before he reaches Saturn, the sixth planet from the Sun. An average distance of 890 million miles (1.4 billion kilometers) separates Earth and the ringed planet. He activates a tiny radio device in his cape to speak with Professor Hamilton.

"You're traveling to the second largest planet in our solar system," says Hamilton.

"Saturn is mostly made up of gases, right?" asks Superman.

"That's correct," says Hamilton. "The four planets closest to the Sun are all rocky with hard surfaces. That includes Mercury, Venus, Earth, and Mars. But Jupiter, Saturn, Uranus, and Neptune are gas giants. Saturn is mostly hydrogen and helium."

FACT

Although Saturn is huge, it's the least dense planet in our solar system. The gases that make up Saturn are not packed very tightly. If you could find an ocean large enough to hold Saturn, the planet would float on top of the water.

"So the planet doesn't have a solid surface to stand on?" asks Superman.

"No, and I'm afraid it won't be a fun place to visit," says Hamilton. "Saturn is very stormy. Fierce winds blow at over 1,100 miles, or 1,800 kilometers, per hour. That's 10 times faster than most hurricanes on Earth."

"I'm flying over Saturn now," says Superman. "A large area of white clouds is swirling in the northern part of the planet."

"That's a Great White Spot," explains Hamilton. "It's a giant storm that travels around the planet. One forms about every 20 or 30 Earth years."

Superman zooms by an oddly shaped moon. Its surface is covered with thousands of holes.

"Professor, I just passed a moon that looks like a giant sponge!" the hero says.

"That would be Hyperion," replies Hamilton. "It's actually an icy rock covered with deep craters."

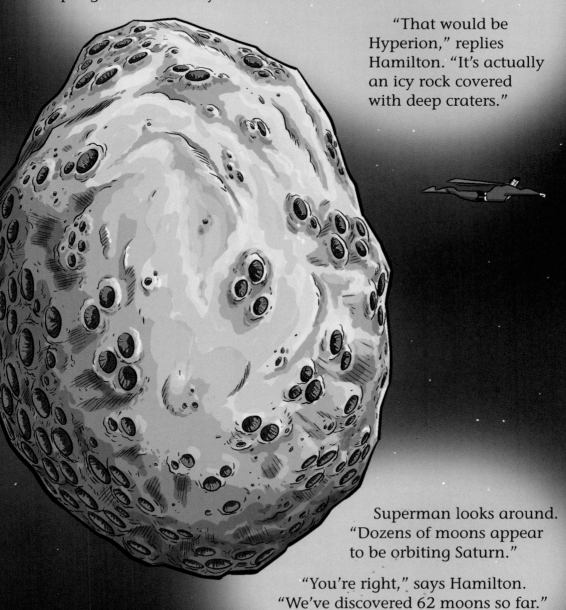

Superman looks around. "Dozens of moons appear to be orbiting Saturn."

"You're right," says Hamilton. "We've discovered 62 moons so far."

"The final image we received from the spacecraft was broadcast somewhere near Titan, the largest of Saturn's moons," says Hamilton.

"I see it in the distance," says Superman. "It's huge!"

"Yes, Titan is even bigger than the planet Mercury," adds Hamilton. "Titan has an atmosphere made mostly of nitrogen. In fact, it's the only moon in our solar system with a thick atmosphere."

Superman zooms through space. "I'm going there now."

FACT
Titan's atmosphere might be similar to what Earth's atmosphere was like billions of years ago. Scientists think Titan may hold clues to how life began on our planet.

Superman drops down through Titan's atmosphere. He flies over the moon's brown, icy surface.

"Titan looks like Earth in many ways," says Hamilton. "It has mountains, sand dunes, riverbeds, and thousands of lakes filled with liquid methane. We think those lakes could be home to some form of life!"

"Professor, I see the spacecraft up ahead!" says Superman.

The Man of Steel lands next to the craft. It has been ripped in half. A sheet of metal is wedged between the two pieces.

"Someone's burned a message into this metal panel," says the Man of Steel. "It's written in the language of Krypton, the planet where I was born. It says, 'Saturn is ours, Superman!'"

"Who could've done this?" asks Hamilton.

"I'm afraid this is the work of villains who must have escaped from the Phantom Zone," says Superman. "It's a Kryptonian prison that exists in another dimension. All Phantom Zone prisoners come from Krypton and have the same powers as me. One of them probably used heat-vision to write the message."

The Man of Steel knows he needs to capture the criminals before they cause any more trouble.

Superman launches high above Titan. He zooms into the bright rings that circle Saturn.

"From far away, the rings look solid," says Hamilton. "But close up, you'll see they're made of billions of pieces of ice. The chunks can be as small as a grain of sand or bigger than a house."

"What makes the rings so bright?" asks Superman.

"The icy particles reflect the sunlight especially well," replies Hamilton. "You can even see the rings from Earth through a small telescope."

FACT
Scientists think Saturn's rings may be the fragments of an icy moon that was torn apart by the planet's gravity. Or the moon may have been smashed into pieces when it collided with another body.

Superman soars through the rings. Chunks of ice bounce off his super-strong body.

Suddenly, the savage Kryptonian super-villain Jax-Ur zooms into view. He draws back his fist and strikes Superman.

"The Phantom Zone could not hold me or my two friends," Jax-Ur says with a harsh laugh. "Prepare to meet your end, Man of Steel!"

FACT
Saturn's ring system is about 175,000 miles (282,000 km) wide, but it's very thin. In some places, the rings are only 30 feet (10 meters) thick.

Superman doubles over in pain. But he quickly recovers and launches himself at Jax-Ur.

The Man of Steel flies in circles around the surprised villain. He travels faster and faster until his foe is dizzy and confused.

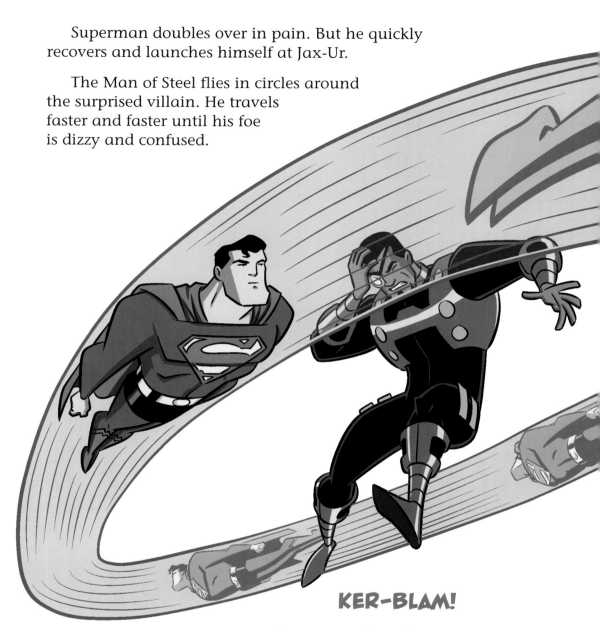

KER-BLAM!

Superman slams his fists against the villain. The punch knocks out Jax-Ur. He floats away into the icy rings.

"That's one Phantom Zone prisoner down," says Superman.

"Professor, I see another moon," says Superman.
"Huge streams of snow are shooting out of its surface."

"That would be Enceladus," says Hamilton. "Enceladus is pulled in a tug of war between the gravity of Saturn and other nearby moons. These forces squeeze and heat up its interior. Water then shoots up through cracks in the moon's surface and immediately freezes. Some geysers spray ice so high it becomes part of Saturn's rings."

FACT
An ocean of salt water lies beneath the thick, icy crust of Enceladus (pronounced en-SELL-uh-dis). Scientists think these waters could contain some form of life.

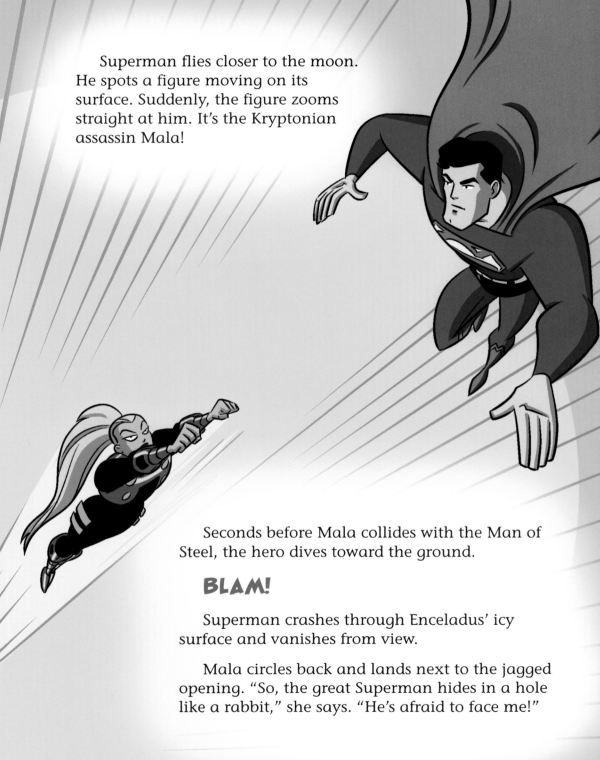

Superman flies closer to the moon. He spots a figure moving on its surface. Suddenly, the figure zooms straight at him. It's the Kryptonian assassin Mala!

Seconds before Mala collides with the Man of Steel, the hero dives toward the ground.

BLAM!

Superman crashes through Enceladus' icy surface and vanishes from view.

Mala circles back and lands next to the jagged opening. "So, the great Superman hides in a hole like a rabbit," she says. "He's afraid to face me!"

WHOOOOSH!

An explosion of ice shoots out of the hole. Before Mala can move, the blast covers her in thick ice.

Superman bursts through the moon's frozen surface. He tricked Mala into coming near a geyser that was about to erupt. He quickly uses his super-breath to add another layer of ice to his frozen foe.

"That's two Phantom Zone villains down," says Superman. "But I have a feeling the worst is still to come."

The Man of Steel flies away. "Professor, I'm going to Saturn now. It looks like the planet is bulging out in the middle."

"That's right. Saturn rotates very fast, about once every 10 and a half hours," says Hamilton. "This causes the equator to bulge outward, where the speed is greatest. The poles also flatten, giving Saturn something of an oval shape."

"I also see a strange six-sided pattern at the north pole," adds Superman.

"That's a giant hurricane," says Hamilton. "We've been studying it since the 1980s. It's 50 times larger than the biggest hurricanes on Earth. The winds whip around and form the hexagon-shaped pattern in the clouds."

Superman soars through the frozen yellow clouds that surround Saturn. Then he drops deeper into the planet's atmosphere.

"Get ready to encounter some major storms and frigid temperatures," warns Hamilton. "It'll likely be around minus 200 degrees Fahrenheit, or minus 130 degrees Celsius."

Giant gusts of wind slam into Superman. It takes all his super-strength to keep moving.

A lightning bolt shoots past the Man of Steel
as an electrical storm rages around him.

CRACK!

"Be careful, Superman," says Hamilton. "Those lightning
bolts are thousands of times more powerful than the ones on
Earth. And electrical storms can last for months on Saturn."

Even with his superpowers, the Man of Steel shivers from
the extreme cold.

A deep voice rings out from within the murky atmosphere.

"So, Superman," it says. "You have found me."

The Man of Steel spins around and sees General Zod floating among the stormy clouds. Zod was the former commander of the Kryptonian army, and he's now one of the most dangerous criminals in the universe.

"Zod! How did you and the others escape from the Phantom Zone?" asks Superman.

"It was easy," says Zod, sneering. "A star exploded—I believe you Earthlings call it a supernova—in a galaxy far away. The blast ripped a hole in the Phantom Zone, setting us free."

FACT
All stars eventually die. The largest go out with a big bang. They expand and then explode in a powerful, spectacular flash of light called a supernova.

"Now I will rule your puny solar system," says Zod. "I have started with Saturn. Soon I will conquer Earth."

"Think again, Zod," says Superman.

The Man of Steel blows an arctic gust of ice at the villain with his super-breath. But Zod activates his heat-vision. The red-hot lasers blast the ice and shoot toward the Man of Steel.

Superman smiles. "I was hoping you would do that."

The super hero holds up his hands. The rays bounce off them and speed back toward Zod. They smash into the villain and send him tumbling backward.

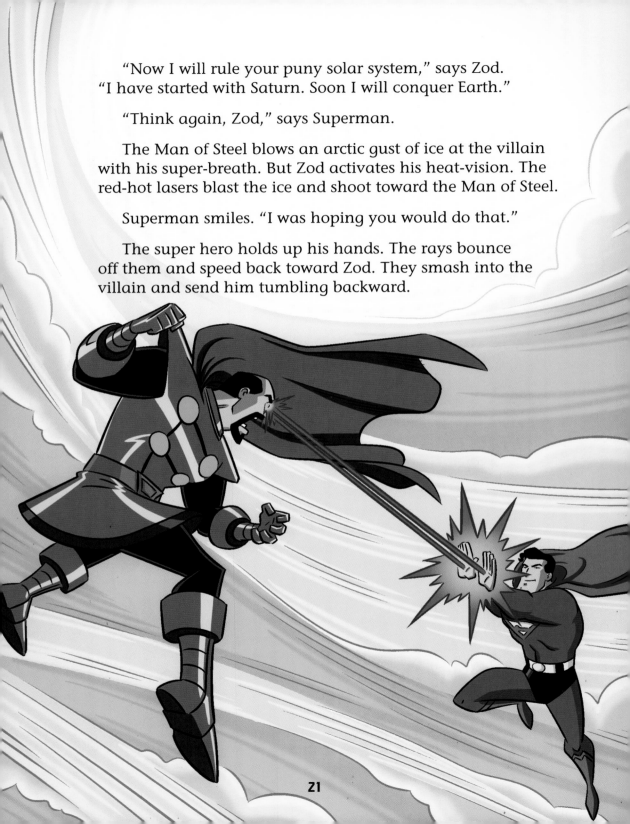

Suddenly, the sound of harsh laughter comes from above. Superman looks up to see Jax-Ur and Mala flying down through Saturn's atmosphere.

"Three against one," says Zod as he moves closer to the Man of Steel. "And we all share the same superpowers. What do you plan to do now?"

ZOOM!

Superman flies away from the three super-villains as fast as he can.

Superman flies to Titan and lands next to the broken S.T.A.R. Labs spacecraft. A white dog in a bright red cape hovers by the hero and wags his tail. It's Krypto the Super-Dog. Krypto can fly and has many superpowers.

"Good boy, Krypto," says Superman to his canine friend. "Thanks for answering my call."

Professor Hamilton's voice sounds over the radio. "Superman, why is Krypto with you? What are you planning?"

"You're about to find out," says Superman as he spots the three villains approaching. "Wish us luck, Professor."

Jax-Ur and Mala rush toward the cold surface of Titan.

"It will be a pleasure to crush you, Man of Steel!" Jax-Ur growls.

Before the criminal can make a move, Superman reaches into the spacecraft and grabs a small machine.

ZAAAAP!

ZAAAAP!

Two rays of bright white light shoot out of the device and surround Jax-Ur and Mala.

Seconds later, the villains vanish.

Zod zooms over. He angrily stares at the empty spot where Jax-Ur and Mala had been hovering.

"How did you—" he begins to ask. Superman quickly pushes a button on the machine.

A blast of light covers Zod.

"*Nooo!*" yells the villain as he fades from view.

Superman sighs with relief. "Mission accomplished, Professor," he says. "The three villains are back in the Phantom Zone."

"I don't understand," says Hamilton. "How did you do that?"

"This machine is a Phantom Zone projector," says Superman. "It sends people to the prison. As soon as I realized I was dealing with Kryptonian criminals, I used my radio to contact Krypto. I asked him to fetch the projector from my Fortress of Solitude and bring it to Titan."

"I'd say that's a very good dog!" says Hamilton with a laugh.

Superman pets his trusty friend and says, "I agree. Come on, Krypto. Let's go home."

"Woof!" adds Krypto.

Soon, Superman and his canine companion soar high above Titan and head back to Earth.

MORE ABOUT SATURN

- In 1610 the Italian astronomer Galileo Galilei used the newly invented telescope to become the first person to observe Saturn's rings. He didn't realize they were rings, though. He thought they might be two large moons on either side of the planet.

- Saturn is named after the Roman god of farming.

- A year on Saturn—the amount of time it takes the planet to orbit the Sun—equals about 30 Earth years.

- Saturn is so far away from the Sun that it receives little sunlight. However, the planet has a very hot core. Scientists estimate the core reaches temperatures of 22,000 degrees Fahrenheit (11,700 degrees Celsius).

- Saturn's seven main rings are named alphabetically in order of their discovery. In order of their distance from the planet, the rings are DCBAFGE.

- Gaps separate many of Saturn's rings, such as the Cassini Division between rings B and A. There's less material in the gaps, which is why they appear empty from a distance.

- Saturn was once thought to be the only planet with rings. That ended in the 1970s and 1980s when astronomers first saw the much darker rings that surround the other three gas giant planets.

- The Cassini-Huygens mission was a joint project between NASA, the European Space Agency, and the Italian Space Agency. *Cassini* was the first spacecraft to study Saturn and its moons up close. It was launched in 1997, but its journey to the gas giant took seven years.

- *Cassini* sent a probe called *Huygens* down to the surface of the moon Titan. The probe sent photos and data for about 90 minutes.

- *Cassini* orbited Saturn for 13 years. It sent more than 450,000 images to NASA. In 2017 scientists ended the craft's mission and plunged it into Saturn's atmosphere. *Cassini* continued to collect and send data until it was destroyed by heat and pressure.

GLOSSARY

asteroid (AS-tuh-royd)—a large space rock that moves around the Sun

astronomer (uh-STRAH-nuh-muhr)—a scientist who studies stars, planets, and other objects in space

atmosphere (AT-muhss-fihr)—the layer of gases that surrounds some planets, dwarf planets, and moons

core (KOR)—the inner part of a planet or moon that is made of metal or rock

crater (KRAY-tuhr)—a hole made when asteroids and comets crash into a planet's or moon's surface

galaxy (GAL-uhk-see)—a large group of stars and planets

geyser (GYE-zur)—an underground spring that shoots hot liquid and steam through a hole in the ground

gravity (GRAV-uh-tee)—a force that pulls objects together

orbit (OR-bit)—to travel around an object in space; also the path an object follows while circling another object in space

solar system (SOH-lur SISS-tuhm)—the Sun and the objects that move around it

supernova (soo-per-NOH-vuh)—the explosion of a huge star at the end of its life that gives off tremendous amounts of energy

READ MORE

Austen, Mary. *Exploring Saturn.* Journey Through Our Solar System. New York: KidHaven Publishing, 2018.

Radomski, Kassandra. *The Secrets of Saturn.* North Mankato, Minn.: Capstone Press, 2016.

Royston, Angela. *The Cassini Mission: Robots Exploring Saturn and Its Moon Titan.* Robots Exploring Space. New York, Powerkids Press, 2016.

TITLES IN THIS SET

INTERNET SITES

Use FactHound to find Internet sites related to this book.
Visit *www.facthound.com*
Just type in 9781543515725 and go.

Published by Capstone Press in 2018
1710 Roe Crest Drive
North Mankato, Minnesota 56003
www.mycapstone.com

Cataloging-in-publication information is on file with the Library of Congress.
ISBN 978-1-5435-1572-5 (library binding)
ISBN 978-1-5435-1580-0 (paperback)
ISBN 978-1-5435-1588-6 (eBook PDF)

Editorial Credits
Abby Huff, editor; Kyle Grenz, designer; Laura Manthe, production specialist

Summary: Superman is rounding up General Zod and other escaped Kryptonian criminals and
along the way will discover remarkable features and characteristics of Saturn and its moons.

Illustration Credits
Dario Brizuela: front cover, back cover (space), 1 (space), 28–29, 30–31, 32 (space)

Printed in the United States of America